Lauri M. Nelson

Connect & Win

How to Build Value
with the Service of Selling

Editor: Jen Juneau
Cover and interior design: Oana Rafaila

ISBN 978-0-578-70120-2

LauriMNelson.com

Dedicated to my Mama
Mother Minnie Mae Nelson
10/19/1940 – 4/30/2020

ACKNOWLEDGMENTS

I'm so grateful and appreciative to have such an awesome support system. Having people in your life who love you unconditionally and always want the best for you—people who tend to ask you the tough questions, always encourage you at the right time, give you their time even when it's not convenient for them, and support and nourish both you and your gifts—is truly a blessing.

Special thanks to my support system. Your contributions, even if you think they were small (they weren't), helped to make this book possible:

Danica Smith

Aretha Simons

Jean Scott Smith

Salathia Nelson

Tabitha Nelson

Shayla Dougher

Terry Newmyer

Charlene Aldrich

Gocha Hawkins

Qiana Johnson

If I missed your name, please charge it to my head and not my heart.

CONTENTS

Introduction

A great sales job is still one of the most sought-after careers. Why? Whether selling for yourself or someone else, it's one of the fastest ways to positively change your financial future. If it's done properly, you can make a lot of money, learn a skill you can use anywhere at any age, and change lives for the better. Also, if executed correctly, it comes with some responsibility: the responsibility of being a servant, by putting yourself aside to really listen to and understand how to be of the most benefit to your client. If you become their servant by listening, displaying empathy, and understanding their unique situation, it's a guarantee that your reward will far exceed your sales commission.

The objective of this short book is to share with you an underutilized communication technique that, once applied, will provide you with winning sales tactics to help you become more successful not only in sales but in your day-to-day interactions outside of work. After reading, you'll have tools you can employ immediately, offering you quicker successes.

For more than fifteen years, I've had the pleasure of honing my communication and sales skills in various industries. My support and sales assignments have spanned operations management, engineering, pharmaceuticals, medical devices, business-to-business (B2B) account management with elite medical and teaching institutions, real-estate investing, fitness and nutrition, and business-to-consumer (B2C) education. Throughout those many assignments, one central theme persisted: I was able to explore and evolve in my God-given gift of communication.

During many of my assignments, the organizations offered a different sales method and pitch strategy to learn and implement. My sales-training matrix consists of consultative selling, DISC selling, SPIN selling—you name it, I've done it. Most sales models have similar themes, but what I've come to learn is that you can teach or train to any sales model on the planet, but if that teaching or training isn't effectively deployed by the organization or embraced by the intended user, it becomes useless and money not well spent.

In all of my roles, I was eager to learn as much as possible. Throughout the early stages of my career (as a junior rep, in some cases) and even some later engagements, I was exposed to those who were reluctant to "toe the company line" of training. In hindsight, I wonder if committing to a sales model or just winging one's sales discussion is financially rewarding and beneficial.

Just kidding—of course, committing and executing on a proven model would reap dividends for the sales representative, the organization, and the customer. But how much value goes undelivered, and how much money is left on the table when we "wing it"?

Therein lies the opportunity. If an organization isn't promoting continuous training of its sales representatives on their sales model, the representative isn't delivering on the sales model, and the sales model isn't designed to uncover the prospect's true goals, then it (and they) will fail, hard. The most important element of a sales model should be to uncover, or create, a need or an opportunity, then work to resolve or improve a situation by showcasing how your product or service can fill that gap better than another product or service. This type of model creates a win, a win for your client and yourself.

Oftentimes, when sales goals are missed, management tends to place blame on their sales representatives for not being aggressive or hungry enough. On the other end of the spectrum, sales representatives make excuses or place blame on management for everything from poor product mix to bad company leadership to inadequate field training or even, not enough training.

Enough of the blame game. Management must take responsibility for its training programs' effectiveness or lack thereof and methods for helping its field force be accountable, while sales professionals must take responsibility for showing up eager every day, executing the plan diligently, and self-assessing to identify weak spots and seek support for performance improvement. Winning takes teamwork and, more importantly, the proper training, as well as a willingness and dedication to execute.

Another thing winning requires is a caring attitude. Attempting to promote a product you're lifeless about will put you, and subsequently the organization, on the losing end. If you can't get behind your product and your skills and sales training leave room for improvement, it can breed apathy, laziness, and limited success, as well as further perpetuate the fallacy that corporate sales models don't work. Often, a sales model not working effectively is simply a matter of not putting training to the test with dedication and heart.

So, let's take a trip together to uncover some valuable tools to help you and/or your teams get on the same page, communicate more effectively, and close more sales.

In order to maintain anonymity, names of companies and employees have been changed.

CHAPTER 1

Care to Win

Many years ago, I was working on a school project. It was a marketing assignment. We had to select an industry, then an organization within that industry to research and identify areas where they could grow their market presence. Our direction was to provide strategic guidance, as well as implementation tactics. During my research on the construction industry, I learned there was a need for more active senior-living communities, so I focused on a top home builder. The project outcome was a hit with my instructor. Subsequently, I wanted to share my findings with the then-CEO of the homebuilding company.

I ended up mailing my marketing research to the company headquarters via United States Priority Mail. In big red letters across the envelope was written CONFIDENTIAL. I tracked the package and, seeing it had arrived, called the company's headquarters and asked the CEO's secretary if I could speak with the CEO. I could only imagine what the secretary was thinking. I inquired if the package had been delivered and the secretary said yes, and that the CEO would eventually get it. I explained to her that the package contained important information and I really needed to speak with him about it personally. She said that speaking with him was unlikely and he would get it eventually and review it.

The next day, I called back asking the same thing. Again, she stated he would get it eventually and take a look. This went on for three days. On the fourth day, I told her it was imperative that the CEO got the package that day, as it held time-sensitive information with major ramifications for his business. She then patched me through—wow!

Check Out the Call

CEO: "Hello?"

Me: "Hello, Mr. Jones. Thank you for taking my call."

CEO: "How did you get through my secretary?"

Me: "I told her that it was imperative that we speak today, as the future of your organization lies in the package I sent you early this week." (I went on to explain my findings.)

CEO: "Okay. I have your package here. Thank you for this information. Is that it?"

Me: "Yes, that's it. Have a great day."

You're probably wondering, "You did all of that to talk to the CEO of a major organization with no additional ask?" Yep. I had one mission in mind, and it was accomplished. But later, after I realized the magnitude of what happened, I kicked myself because I should've planned better for the call or

> Always do my Pre-Call Planning. Know what I'm going in for and have a plan to get it or get closer to it.

had a bigger ask in mind. Has that ever happened to you? I guess it's all part of the growing process.

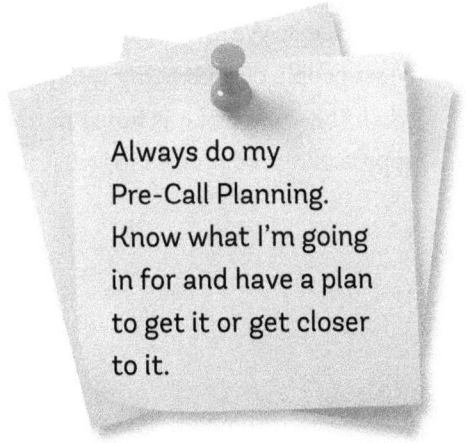

As time passed, I thought about the secretary and hoped she didn't get fired. Surprisingly enough, that homebuilder did add more active senior-living communities across the US. Was that because of the strategy presented to him? I can't be certain, but I felt good about the entire process, nonetheless.

What did I really learn from that interaction with the secretary and CEO of the top homebuilder in the US? In sales, and even in life, if you care more about the one you're serving and the customer can sense that—in my case, the customer was the secretary—accomplishing your goals is doable and, in some cases, even easy.

> Do I care enough? How can I get even more engaged?

Let's face it: We're all customers at some point in the sales cycle. Most people despise being sold to, but I enjoy it. I especially enjoy when the salesperson is tuned in to my needs and desires and is approaching the process for what it is: a listening experience.

CHAPTER 2

Listening?
I Think Not...

In my role as director of an education center, where we generated leads and educated consumers on a treatment for a medical condition, I became more tolerant of solicited (and sometimes unsolicited) sales calls. On one occasion, I received a solicited call from a mortgage company as I was looking to refinance a property.

Check Out the Call

Rep: "Hi, I'm trying to reach Lauri."

Me: "Who's calling, please?"

Rep: "This is Delores calling from 123 Lending regarding your inquiry for a refinance."

Me: "This is Lauri. Thanks for calling me. I can't really talk about that right now—can you call me later?"

Fast-Talking Rep: "Well, your inquiry states that you want to close ASAP and in order for us to do that, I'll have to get your information quickly. So, if you have just a few minutes, I can take some basic information now and we can talk again later."

Reluctant Me: "Sure. What information do you need?"

(Twenty minutes later, after answering some detailed application questions...)

Rep: "You should also know that we have the lowest closing fees."

Me: "Okay, great. I might inquire with other companies, just as due diligence."

Rep: "Well, you can check with other companies, but whatever they tell you might not be complete information. You won't get all the details until you finalize the application."

Me: "Okay. That's fine, but I'm likely to check with more anyway."

Rep: "Well, you should know that we have the highest standard in the industry, and we won't sell your loan like other companies."

Me: "Great, but that's not a critical factor for me."

Rep: "We also have great customer ratings." (Blah blah blah...)

Frustrated Me: "You know what? That's okay. I'm no longer interested. We can stop here. I'll find another company to work with."

Where did this representative go wrong? She failed to listen to me—and not only that, she even failed to ask me any valid questions to help me know she cared about my journey. Do you think I used this person or even this mortgage company? No, I didn't, but you already knew that.

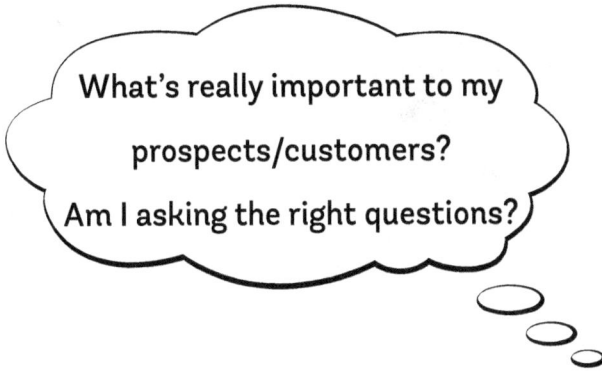

> What's really important to my prospects/customers?
>
> Am I asking the right questions?

The above example is just a snapshot of what can happen on sales calls. I'm almost certain you've had one if not more similar experiences, as this is a challenge area in most industries: effective communication from phone staff.

Another industry where phone communication skills could use an up-lift is telecommunications. As more people have moved or are moving to streaming services, cable companies are working to find ways to stabilize and grow their revenue—and rightly so. I personally began streaming not only to avoid the rising cost of cable service but because I was rarely home to enjoy its "benefits," so it seemed to be a waste of my resources. I've been cable-free for many years now and have saved hundreds, if not thousands, of dollars doing it.

Over my years of streaming and simply being an internet customer, I've received a few calls about upgrading my service plan. One call in particular, that I politely accepted, solidified a thought in me that some, if not most, organizations could benefit from more effective sales training of their staff.

Check Out the Call

Me: "Hello?"

Rep: "Hello, can I speak with Lauri Nelson?"

Me: "Who's calling, please?"

Rep: "This is Brice calling from 123 Cable Company."

Me: "This is Lauri."

Rep: "Great! Lauri, I noticed that you've been a long-time customer and that you're only using our internet service. We're offering a special plan where you can get bundled services of phone, cable, and internet for a small increase in your monthly bill, allowing you to enjoy the benefits of all services. You can also stream on any device, while at home or away, whenever you desire, without any additional costs."

Me: "Thank you, but I'm not interested in changing plans, and—"

Rep: "But ma'am, you could get access to any television show that you want on any device you want."

Me: "But you aren't hearing what I'm saying. I don't watch much television and—"

Rep: "Ma'am, do you have a smartphone? Because you could stream television or even Netflix to your smartphone at any time."

Me: "Okay. I'm good with the plan that I have."

Rep: "Ma'am, are you sure? Because—"

Me: "Listen, I answered the call politely. I don't want to be rude, but I'm hanging up the phone now, okay? I'm good with my current plan. Goodbye."

What happened here? He could've asked me a more relevant probing question. He could've asked several probing questions, but he was trained to, what I call, "message vomit"—and he did just that.

Message Vomit— Giving a sales presentation or pitch without stopping to ask questions or check in on your prospect.

Given the plethora of organizations with in-house sales teams that handle sales calls via phone, having the right skills to build rapport quickly should be goal No. 1! For organizations that don't train their employees to build rapport quickly and effectively, especially in call centers, there awaits waste from unconverted leads, low employee morale, and diminished returns on investments, (ROI).

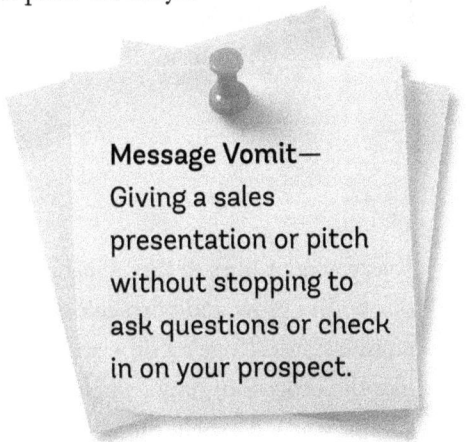

CHAPTER 3

Processes, Processes, Processes, Oh My

Every area of life's dealings has a process. There's a process of how our bodies grow and burn calories. There's a process of how a car engine starts. There's a process of how we make decisions—like the process of how you chose to purchase and read this book (thank you!). As such, there's a basic process of building rapport, demonstrating value, and/or selling—and, if executed correctly, it always starts with communication between at least two parties. Ideally, one party is seeking (knowingly or not) and one is serving.

Most sales models follow a general pattern, as shown below:

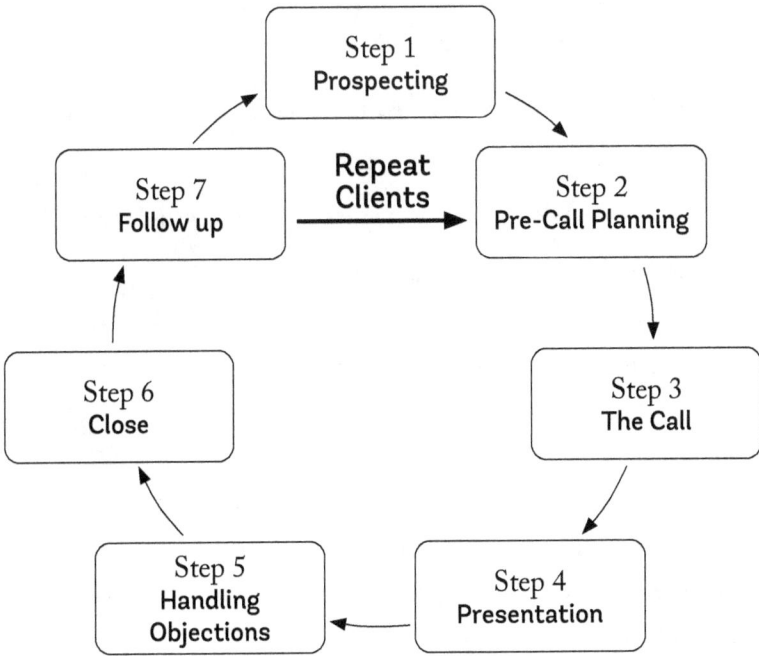

```
                    ┌─────────────────┐
                    │     Step 1      │
                    │   Prospecting   │
                    └─────────────────┘
   ┌──────────────┐   Repeat    ┌─────────────────────┐
   │   Step 7     │   Clients   │       Step 2        │
   │   Follow up  │ ──────────► │  Pre-Call Planning  │
   └──────────────┘             └─────────────────────┘

   ┌──────────────┐             ┌─────────────────────┐
   │   Step 6     │             │       Step 3        │
   │    Close     │             │      The Call       │
   └──────────────┘             └─────────────────────┘

   ┌──────────────┐             ┌─────────────────────┐
   │   Step 5     │ ◄────────── │       Step 4        │
   │   Handling   │             │    Presentation     │
   │  Objections  │             └─────────────────────┘
   └──────────────┘
```

Step 1: Prospecting—Basically finding potential customers and generating qualified leads.

Step 2: Pre-Call Planning—Research your potential customer (or review notes from your last conversation) to identify their potential gaps and how your offering might fill the gaps. Final review of the presentation typically happens at this stage, as well.

Step 3: The Call—Customer contact is made. One would usually conduct small talk, as appropriate, and then ask questions to identify the client's true gaps and desires, whether known or unknown.

Step 4: Presentation—The salesperson shares the features and benefits of their product or service and hopefully lines up their offering with the customer's desires.

Step 5: Handling Objections—At this point, any questions or concerns are addressed.

Step 6: Close—Ask for the business. Review prices and terms.

Step 7: Follow up—Connect with the customer to ensure they're satisfied and, if appropriate, ask for a referral from the customer. For repeat calls to the same client, redeploy Steps 2 through 7.

The above model works well in most cases. The process is proven effective time and again. The real challenge with representatives not closing sales with the above process is not the steps themselves but what happens *within* those critical steps. In the two interactions I shared previously, both sales representatives knew I was a qualified lead because I reached out to the mortgage company and the cable company knew my buying history. Steps 1 and 2 were completed for them.

Step 3 is where the calls fell apart. There were no probing questions asked, and if no probing questions are asked, how can you hear what the customer **truly** wants or desires? How can you learn where the true gaps are and how to fit your product or service effectively into their world? If you don't ask **thoughtful** questions and listen, how do you help the customer know you're there for them—that you're there solely to help them overcome whatever gap presents itself?

"People do not care how much you know until
they know how much you care."
Unknown

As an education-center director, my past engineering and, more
importantly, service and sales background helped us create
a very effective program. From writing the copy to creating
our model for service and sales execution and providing the
onboarding and training for our teams; it proved to be a winning
combination. Our efforts resulted in a lead-to-paying-customer
conversion rate of 32%. The service delivery was in the life-science
space, where conversion rates of 10 to 20% are typical.[1] Our
performance showed a 60% conversion increase from the top. Most
organizations would be thrilled with conversion rates of that scale.

Additionally, the team's execution was so effective that the program
service delivery was perceived as "World Class" by our customers
based on post-purchase surveys (Step 7), using the Net Promoter
Score (NPS).[2]

Learning of the energy, time, and finances required to invest in
generating leads, it became very clear to me that strategic planning
to lead generation required a strategic and tactical plan to nurture
and convert. Without a cohesive plan and the skills to carry through,
an organization creates a significant waste of time and unnecessarily
bleeds through financial resources, all of which can be avoided. This
is the reason I'm sharing what I know, as it can be highly beneficial
to many if properly implemented and executed, as it was for me and
my team.

CHAPTER 4

Rapport

How did my team achieve such success in sales and service delivery? The answer is in the sales model we used, which is the same as what we discussed in the previous chapter. However, our model included a slight modification.

If you recall, the process steps can be the same for many models, but what's critical is what happens within those steps. If you or your organization are able to generate qualified leads, you're way ahead of the game. Now, what do you do with them? How do you help them fulfill their need or desire to purchase from you? How do you convert them to clients?

> In this noisy environment, what am I doing to differentiate myself or differentiate the conversation?

Using a combination of word choice and a proven model or framework to communicating can help one be a better listener, communicate more effectively, display empathy, build better relationships overall, and get in alignment with the one they're speaking with. So why not combine the two—**word choice** and **framework**—when working to nurture and convert leads, or training our teams?

Word choice and a proven framework, when used appropriately, can aid in the process of rapport building: a valuable element to the inner workings of a successful sales process. Rapport building goes deeper than 'You like to fish and so do I.' Rapport building is about truly connecting with people and is often the missing key in sales models and presentations and was certainly missing in my two encounters above.

Why do we, as sales professionals, believe that a specific sales model won't yield success? I've heard seasoned sales professionals make some of the following statements:

- *Corporate can't tell me how to sell my product.*
- *I've been selling this bag for years. I know more about selling than anyone in-house would ever know.*
- *I'm not going to use this model. My customers will view me as fake and weak for toeing the company line.*
- *My customers deserve for me to be myself when I talk to them.*
- *The product will sell itself.*
- *The customer already knows everything about my product. There's nothing else to say.*

The list goes on and on. No doubt these thoughts and behaviors are passed down from sales rep to sales rep, perpetuating a fallacy about sales-model ineffectiveness. In my many years of selling, I've come to believe that if a model is hard to understand and implement and there are no examples of its success, it will not be adopted. Instilling a process to cross a raging river is vital to success, and to our existence. Having the right stones in the water to step on makes the journey less precarious and emboldens those you lead to follow. As is true in life, so is true in sales; Proven success of the model's tactics makes those who follow more eager and excited for the journey.

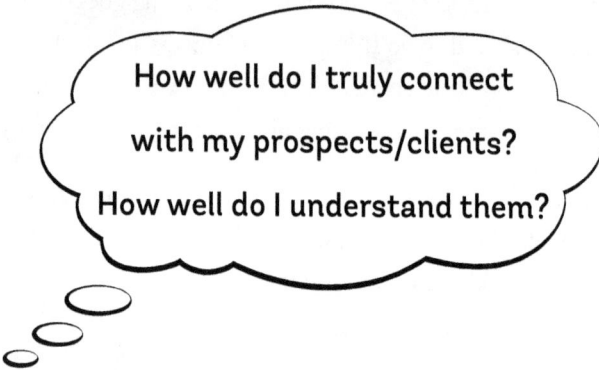

> **How well do I truly connect with my prospects/clients? How well do I understand them?**

CHAPTER 5

NLP: Cleared for Launch!

A method of rapport building called neuro-linguistic programming (NLP) is the model that was incorporated and successfully executed with my team. According to GoodTherapy.org, NLP "is a psychological approach that involves analyzing strategies used by successful individuals and applying them to reach a personal goal. It relates thoughts, language, and patterns of behavior learned through experience to specific outcomes."[3] There are many facets of NLP focused on various parts of human behavior and self-improvement. However, my goal will be to share a subset here, which you can apply quickly to improve your sales and communication skills.

NLP as a communication and rapport-building technique was introduced in the 1970s and is a body of work that expanded quickly, given its focus on self-improvement.[3] There are naysayers of the NLP framework who throw stones at its transformative soundness and don't believe the model works. However, the tactics you'll learn in this book have been proven to work, and with any process, you only get out what you put in. Some of the most successful and effective communicators of our time employ NLP as a rapport-building technique. Stated practitioners of NLP methods include Oprah Winfrey, Tony Robbins, and many more perceived users.[4]

Here's what they've stated about the valuable technique:

> "NLP helps me to manage audiences and motivate them. It is amazing."
> *Oprah Winfrey*

> "I built my sales career from zero to become the world's best motivator using NLP."
> *Tony Robbins*

My introduction to NLP as a rapport-building and sales technique came during my deep dive into the field of health and wellness. My mentor was Lucho Crisalle, a master of the NLP technique, and I'm grateful for the valuable guidance he provided me in becoming a more effective communicator.

In NLP, there are various segments, or modalities, to consider. For our purposes, we'll cover the VAK System (Visual, Auditory, Kinesthetic) and Meta Programs, as you'll be able to implement them with ease and drive results quickly. As you incorporate this subset of NLP into your day-to-day practice, you may want to add more segments to become even more effective. Just know that what I'm going to share with you here has been proven to work.

There are multiple books and hundreds of articles about NLP, and if you do a Google search on it, you'll find over 25 pages of unique websites. Most resources highlight similar information: what NLP is. **The purpose of this book is to share with you how to apply this effective sales and rapport building technique quickly and easily.** So, if you're looking for a dissertation on the topic or a resource covering every detail, you'll need to buy another book. But if you want to take the opportunity to quickly understand a proven tactic to communicate better, close more sales, and grow your business, keep reading.

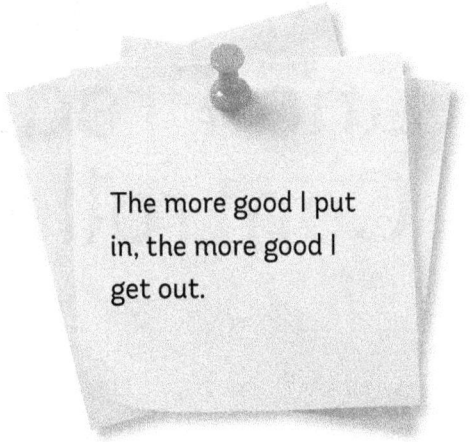

> The more good I put in, the more good I get out.

Let me give you fair warning before we start our fly-by: What do Oprah Winfrey, Tony Robbins, former President Bill Clinton, and others who use the NLP approach have in common? They're all great listeners. Sorry to ruin this for you, but you must at least be willing to listen in order to properly incorporate any rapport-building technique, especially NLP, effectively.

And don't worry if your listening skills have room for improvement. I'm going to help you learn to listen better. I've done it for others, and I can do it for you. Let's go!

CHAPTER 6.

VAK Formula and Predicates: Controlled Dive

One facet of NLP focuses on how people make decisions. How valuable would it be if you knew how your most sought-after leads or prospects best received information and made decisions? This is what the VAK (Visual, Auditory, Kinesthetic) system is all about.

Usually, people operate in more than one modality, and knowing the sequence or dominant method in which they best receive information and make decisions is your objective. Having this information allows you to communicate with your prospect more effectively and build rapport, through pacing their behavior at a quicker and higher level. There are numerous combinations in which the VAK modality, or predicates, can present themselves. Your objective is to *listen* and determine what the combination is. Once you learn a prospect's combination or dominant mode of processing information, you can help move the conversation forward in a mutually beneficial way.

> Do I really know how my prospects/clients best receive information to make decisions?

Of our five senses, we primarily use three to process information:

- Sight/Visual (V)—Information is processed best when seen.
- Hearing/Auditory (A)—Information is processed best when heard.
- Touch or Feel/Kinesthetic (K)—Information is processed best with hands-on experience or how one feels.

Taste and smell are important as well but to a lesser degree, for the majority of us humans, when processing information.

Some possible VAK combinations are VVV, VAA, VKK, VKA, AAK, KKA, KVV, AKA, and so on. However, you only care about the combination of the person in front of you. Listen and it will reveal itself.

For this information to be revealed, you'll likely have to ask a probing question. Sometimes the question is as simple as, "How may I assist you?" or, "How did you go about making the decision to contact us?"

A prospect's response could be:

> "I **heard** you're offering discounts on your imported blends, so I wanted to **get a feel** of the product to **see** if it's for me."

This person's response combination is Auditory ("heard"), Kinesthetic ("get a feel"), Visual ("see"): AKV.

How about this one?

> **Rep:** "Hello, how can I assist you?"
>
> **Customer:** "I was just walking through the outlet and had a feeling to come in and look around."

This person's response combination is Kinesthetic ("walking through"), Kinesthetic ("feeling"), Visual ("look"): KKV.

Once you learn the person's formula for communicating, your objective is to mirror them to build trust and rapport, quicker. For example, a salesperson's response could be:

> **Rep:** "Thanks so much. **Feel** free to **hang out**. If you **see** something you like, just let me know."

This rep followed with a K ("feel") K ("hang out") V ("see") response and matched the customer's communication style. Rapport was built immediately, and both parties moved closer to creating a mutually beneficial relationship.

When asking probing questions, you can sometimes get an earful. If so, what a wonderful blessing when you know how to handle it. But often, when one is flatfooted and out of sync with their prospect, this may lead them to think, "Oh, my, I forgot their first, second, third—oh wow, a *fourth*—predicate. What do I do now?"

Not to worry—modalities can be delivered in more than threes (and they often are, because most people operate on a continuum of modalities), but your objective is to **listen with purpose** for a person's dominant modality, in the event you're given an autobiography.

Look at this example:

> **Rep:** "Hello. What brings you in today?"
>
> **Customer:** "I **saw** the sale sign, then I **heard** the ad on the radio, and my friend **spoke** with me about a very **soft** and beautiful blanket she purchased here, and I was **speechless** over how much she paid. So please **tell** me about this sale because I need more linens and blankets for family coming to visit for the holiday and, as usual, I want them to be comfortable and have a great time."

This person gave you a great deal of information, which is wonderful and very helpful if you know what to listen for and then, more importantly, what to do with it. What is this person's sequence? What is the dominant modality of this individual?

This person's response is VAAKAA: Visual ("saw"), Auditory ("heard"), Auditory ("spoke"), Kinesthetic ("soft"), Auditory ("speechless"), Auditory ("tell").

Auditory is their dominant modality, because A's are the majority. Based on this information, you should focus your presentation in the auditory realm, delivering points that resonate with the prospect's auditory and hearing function. Imagine presenting a very touchy-feely, kinesthetic presentation to an auditory person. MAJOR FAIL!

Your response could go something like this:

> **Rep:** "Let me **tell** you, this sale is huge, so I totally understand. Many people **heard** about it and have come in to buy needed blankets and other linens. What more can you **tell** me about your friend's blanket? Maybe I can **tell** you where it is in the store or even take you to where it **sounds** like that type of blanket could be stocked."

The representative's response focused on the customer's dominant **Auditory** communication style, allowing rapport to build quickly and organically. The response also used other features of NLP that we'll cover in the next chapter.

What's your VAK formula? How would you answer similar questions above?

Please go to **www.LauriMNelson.com** and take a look at the many resources available. All are there to assist you in gaining a better understanding of these techniques through practical application. As always, excellence in practice helps win the game.

Am I speaking to my customer using their modality or mine?

CHAPTER 7

Meta Programs: Controlled Dive

Another component of NLP focuses on how people are motivated. Since we can't truly motivate someone, knowing *how* one is motivated can be priceless in our work *and* personal lives.

You tell me: How valuable would it be if you knew how your most sought-after prospect was motivated? Again, you can't motivate someone—motivation comes from within, so understanding one's motivations can be immensely beneficial to all parties. When you can ascertain how one is motivated to make decisions, you can then use language to produce a more desirable and favorable outcome. Some might consider this manipulation, but it's not. You're simply using the individual's own characteristics to arrive at a next-step approach.

> How can I inspire my prospect's/client's motivations? Do I know their motivations?

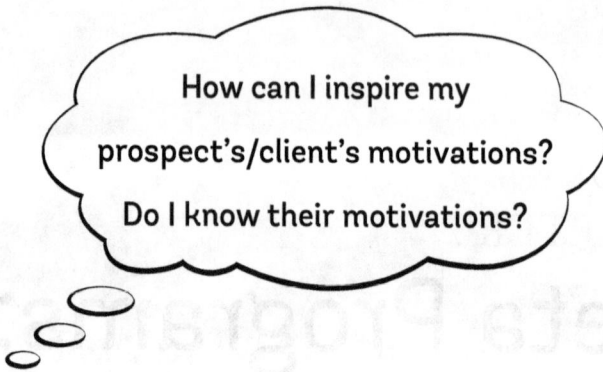

In the macro world of NLP, there are sometimes seven, eight, or even eleven Meta Programs discussed, depending on your source. For our purposes—better communication and more effective sales tactics—we'll focus on three because, as I've stated before, they've been proven to work and are simple to apply.

The focused Meta Program motivation signals are:

- Necessity or Opportunity (N or O)—A person's Motivation Decision
- Away from Pain or Towards Pleasure (A or T)—A person's Motivation Direction
- Internal or External Frame of Reference (I or E)—A person's Motivation Authority Source

The Meta Programs as stated above are descriptive but allow me to add more context for better understanding.

Motivation Decision

Motivation Decision identifies how people make their decisions—in other words, how are they motivated to decide? The NLP model presumes people make decisions based on **Necessity** or **Opportunity**. One method of deciding is not better than another in any way—it's simply how a person is equipped. This motivator is the most important one to get correct, as misidentifying your prospect's decision pattern can derail your rapport-building process.

Imagine making the following statement to your most sought-after prospect who makes decisions driven by Opportunity:

> "You need to close the deal soon because time is
> not on our side."

How likely is it for her to follow your advice? The likelihood of her responding to that prodding is zero, and she'll likely either dismiss the deal completely or only reconsider it on her timetable. We'll review this a bit more later.

Motivation Direction

In dealing with Motivation Direction, a person's attention is directed either *towards* what they want or *away* from what they don't want. You must be careful and unassuming when delving to uncover this motivation. Often, we can obtain a response that sounds like **Towards Pleasure**, but if you dig a bit deeper, it could actually be **Away from Pain**.

Look at this example:

> **Customer:** "I want to lose weight and look good."
> (Sounds like Towards Pleasure, right?)

People have numerous reasons for wanting to lose weight. The "and look good" portion of the above response is superficial and requires more probing to go deeper and get to the real matter.

> **Rep:** "Why is that important to you?"

> **Customer:** "Because I don't want my wife to leave me."
> (Away from Pain is the true Motivation Direction.)

An easy clue for Motivation Direction is, after **appropriate and sufficient** probing, if you hear the word "don't," the person's direction is Away from Pain. Tony Robbins wrote a great article on this topic, called "Finding the Right Key."[5]

What if the response was this?:

> **Customer:** "Because I have a great life and I want to keep enjoying my life and live it as long as possible."
> (Towards Pleasure)

How deep does my questioning encourage my prospects/clients to go? Do my questions transcend the surface?

Motivation Authority Source

One's Motivation Authority Source identifies whether their decisions are guided by **internal processes or external influences.** Does a woman buy a new car based on her own research or based on a friend's input and/or experience? Does a man get a new haircut because he thinks it would look good on him or because his girlfriend encouraged him to? Choices—and how they're made— really mean something to the mindful and astute listener.

As with the modality of VAK, one's Meta Program consists of a combination of the three elements above: Necessity or Opportunity, Away from Pain or Towards Pleasure, and Internal or External Frame of Reference. However, unlike VAK, only one Meta Program can be used in a sequence, so the combination of outcomes is a bit less. Again, we don't care how many combinations there are—we only care about the combination of the person in front of us at that moment.

The sequence of signals is not critical here. But you may find, as I did, that gathering your information systematically, through appropriate questioning and probing, helps you listen more effectively, store information in its appropriate mental bank, and recall it at ease when needed.

To gather this information, more in-depth probing and rapport building are required. After all, gaining this intimately private-yet-critical information about your prospect is valuable, and any time committed to this area of the process will be well spent when it comes time to ask for their business. Remember, they are seeking and you are serving. This is your servant mode in action. With the right tools using NLP, you can serve them even better.

The type of questions you ask should be designed around responses that fill in the signal gaps:

- Necessity or Opportunity (N or O)
- Away from Pain or Towards Pleasure (A or T)
- Internal or External Frame of Reference (I or E)

Here are two questions that have proven effective to fill in the gaps:

- *"What brings you in today?"*
- *"How did you go about making the decision to come in today?"*

If you're following along, and I trust you are, you may recall that a very similar question was used in the previous chapter—and that wasn't by mistake. Sometimes a single question can give you a lot of detail, filling in many signal gaps.

Let's replay the previous example:

> **Rep:** "Hello. What brings you in today?"
>
> **Customer:** "I saw the sale sign, then I heard the ad on the radio, and my friend spoke with me about a very soft and beautiful blanket she purchased here, and I was speechless over how much she paid. So please tell me about this sale because I need more linens and blankets for family coming to visit for the holiday and, as usual, I want them to be comfortable and have an enjoyable time."

As we stated previously, this person's dominant mode of receiving information is Auditory (VAAKAA: Visual ["saw"],

Auditory ["heard"], Auditory ["spoke"], Kinesthetic ["soft"], Auditory ["speechless"], Auditory ["tell"]).

But what about their motivators?

- Necessity or Opportunity—"…I need more…" = Necessity
- Away from Pain or Towards Pleasure—"…as usual, I want them to be comfortable and have an enjoyable time." = Towards Pleasure
- Internal or External Frame of Reference—"…my friend spoke with me…" = External (She saw and heard the ads but wasn't compelled to act until her friend spoke to her.)

CHAPTER 8

Going Deeper: Filling in the Gaps

The first Meta Program gap of interest to us is the motivating factor around Frame of Reference, Motivation Authority Source. This is probably the easiest signal gap to acquire, as we speak in this language descriptor more often than others. Additionally, with so much information available, we're often compelled to inquire about frames of reference on a regular basis.

For example, suppose you share a new song with a friend. The dialogue might look like this:

> **You:** "Kim, you have to check out this new song by Zebra. It's hot."
>
> **Friend Kim:** "Really? What's the name of the song?"
>
> **You:** "I can't even remember the name. Let me look in my history and find it."

Kim: "How did you learn about it?"

You: "Dominique told me to check it out last night."

BAM! External.

OR

You: "I was online and ran across it."

BAM! Internal.

If your prospect is inclined to make decisions based on something they researched or have firsthand knowledge of, they have an Internal Frame of Reference. If they're more prone to decide based on information shared with them or the experience or influence of another, they have an External Frame of Reference.

Here's another question you could use to uncover this gap:

> "There are various options to consider when trying to solve this challenge. How did you learn about X?"

You could also consider:

> "What solutions have you tried in the past?"

And follow up with:

> "How did you gauge their effectiveness?"

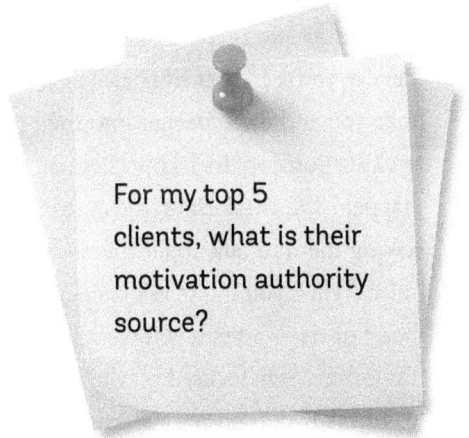

For my top 5 clients, what is their motivation authority source?

When working to identify an Away or Towards position, Motivation Direction, you want to build rapport by getting closer to the core of their pain avoidance or pleasure-seeking motivation.

Here's a helpful question:

> "How has X impacted your life/career/team/ market strategy/growth plans/bottom line?"

Another effective question is:

> "What are you seeking in X?"

Follow up with:

> "Why are you seeking that?"

Remember, your goal is to hear a clear "don't" or a blissful conversation about their desired pleasure, to arrive at the Away from Pain or Towards Pleasure gap filler. Sometimes, the prospect's initial response to your questions could be very surface and superficial. When you believe you're in that situation, be bold and ask a question that can take you and them deeper into their pain avoidance or pleasure-seeking position. In asking these questions, what's the worst that could happen? Oh that's right, the customer might get upset because you're asking them to talk about themselves. Or maybe, you could lose the sale. Well, if you fail to ask deeper probing questions to get to the real heart of the matter, if you don't lose the sale today, you might lose it tomorrow. Stay focused on the fact that you're having this interaction to SERVE the prospect or existing client, so, DELIVER!

> ### What is the unique pain or pleasure driver of my top 5 clients? Do I know?

Sometimes you may find that you don't get all of the responses you're seeking. This is most true for the necessity or opportunity, (N/O), motivator, which is why we usually save this for last, again, if it has not already been revealed. The N/O signal gap is so critical in the process of building and holding rapport that if you fail to get an N or O response after adequate probing, you should ask the question directly.

An example question is:

> "Are you seeking X because you **need** it or because it would be a good **opportunity** for you to Y?"

If a person operates out of Opportunity and you discuss a Necessity motivation with them, you'll break rapport immediately. Sometimes just mentioning need to an opportunity-driven person can upset them, so tread lightly. That observation doesn't hold true in the opposite direction, but your rapport building will initially fall flat. Again, the Motivation Decision is important to assess correctly, as the entire process hinges on using it appropriately.

> How often do I approach my clients from a need perspective? Am I speaking their language or mine?

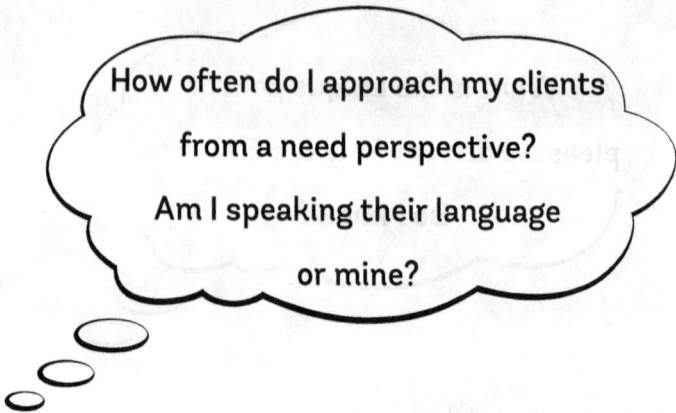

We'll pull all this information together momentarily, allowing you to see how easy and effective it is. Do you know your Meta Programs? How are you motivated?

The beautiful nature of NLP is that it forces you to accept everyone for who they are, as no modality or program is better than another. Everyone is unique and once you understand their uniqueness, you can better present your product or service. All too often, we speak to people based on our communication style. Let's amp up our game and learn to speak with our prospects and clients based on their unique communication style. Believe me, they'll thank you for it!

If you recall, when we started our journey together, I hinted that helping you listen more intently and purposefully and apply the information more effectively was one goal. Listening is not simply about opening your ears and closing your mouth—it's also about knowing what you're listening for. When you know why you're asking a question, it makes you more inclined to listen for the answer as opposed to having an open conversation without a planned intent or next step.

With progressive use and mastery of communication through NLP, your presentations will come off more focused, efficient, and empathetic, because guess what; You're now listening actively, effectively, and purposefully!

In the following chapters, you'll find examples of the NLP framework in action. Also, at www.LauriMNelson.com there are more resources related to Meta Programs to build on your new skill.

CHAPTER 9
The Written Word

Communicating with prospects effectively through written sales copy is just as important as communicating with them verbally, whether face to face or over the phone. Every communication method represents an opportunity to highlight your product or service. When written communication is executed properly, it enhances rapport and builds the bridge to turning a prospect into a satisfied customer.

When communicating via sales copy or email messaging, for example, NLP is a vital tool—in fact, its use can be even more critical with written communications. Why? Email prospecting and selling voids your ability to hear a person's tone or see physical responses to a discussion. Most organizations use language focusing on the features and benefits of their product or service without taking consumer motivations into consideration. However, when sales copy is written with an NLP focus, you combine the latter with features and benefits to create a more compelling catalyst for your prospect to ACT! So how do you write sales copy using NLP that is more likely to capture the attention of your prospects and clients?

As mentioned previously, getting to the point where you can identify your prospect's VAK and Meta Program gets the ball rolling for both you and them. When prospecting via email, as you cannot gather this information, you must write language that covers the three modality receptors and uses all Meta Programs.

Remember, VAK modalities are related to how someone best receives and processes information, while Meta Programs focus on how people are motivated to decide. An effective email messaging campaign should include all motivations and ways of receiving information.

In this email example, let's promote a wellness program:

> Hello, (NAME)! Thank you for taking an opportunity to inquire about our wellness program.
>
> Many people like yourself are looking to get rid of habits that led to being overweight or are frustrated with experiencing the negative effects of high blood pressure, high cholesterol, and diabetes. You can reclaim your life with our simple and proven process. We can help you get leaner, feel even more attractive, and regain the energy and stamina to do the things you enjoy! Whether you've decided to turn your life around yourself or were referred to our program, we can help you.

No need to wait! Call us directly at (888) 555-5555, or click the link below to start a video chat and allow us to walk you through our simple, yet effective program!

As you can see, the email is designed to touch upon Visual ("looking"/"video chat"), Auditory ("call"), and Kinesthetic ("reclaim your life"/"feel"/"walk you through") receptors. Additionally, the Meta Program motivation signals— Away from Pain ("get rid of"), Towards Pleasure ("help you…"), Necessity ("need"), Opportunity ("opportunity"), Internal Frame of Reference ("you've decided"), and External Frame of Reference ("were referred")—are strategically inserted. Writing copy using all aspects discussed creates a large net, encouraging your prospects to jump in and **ACT**!

> Every communication touchpoint is an opportunity to build rapport and add value.

The counterpoint to this method is writing copy devoid of natural response triggers and appropriate motivational drivers. Once your prospect responds to your Call to Action and you're able to have a conversation, you can then ask questions to uncover their unique modality and motivational drivers, allowing you to personalize communication thereafter.

Now that we've covered the written word, let's discuss verbal applications of these concepts: active listening amplified. The following examples are geared towards sales and interview-style questions as they're relatable to most people. However, you should know by now that this framework can apply to any line of questioning in any industry. Rapport building is a requirement if you're promoting your product, your service, or yourself.

CHAPTER 10

The Pen Application

Interviewers looking to hire sales representatives often seek certain abilities during an interview. To gain insight into the level of those abilities during an interview, they sometimes hold out their pen and ask the interviewee, "Please sell me a pen."

I've heard of some interviewees taking the pen and then asking the interviewer to sign their name—as in, "Now that I have your pen, the only way you can sign your name is by buying it back." This would be a FAIL! No one likes to be strong-armed into a sale, no matter how small the deal. It would likely not benefit most hiring managers to have this person on their team, nor is this technique likely to foster an ideal working relationship with a potential client.

Let's go through how an NLP practitioner could approach this question:

Hiring Manager: "Please sell me a pen."

Candidate: "When was the last time you purchased a pen?"

Hiring Manager: "About a month ago?"

Candidate: "What prompted you to make that purchase?"

Hiring Manager: "I was down to my last pen, so I decided I should get some more before I ran out." (Internal Reference)

Candidate: "I totally understand. I've been told that a good salesperson always keeps a pen ready. How did you decide on the brand of pen you purchased?"

Hiring Manager: "I saw an ad and when I went in to check it out, they felt good and did everything I needed, so I purchased them." (VKK and Necessity)

Candidate: "What are you looking for in a pen?"

Hiring Manager: "I don't like pens with a twist-off top—it takes too much time. And when they're heavy, it bothers me because it can hurt my fingers and hand." (Away from Pain)

Candidate: "You like quality merchandise, I can tell. How much would you pay for a pen that fits your needs?"

Hiring Manager: "Oh, I don't know—maybe $15 for an everyday pen."

Candidate: "Well, if I could show you a pen that wasn't heavy and didn't feel uncomfortable in your hand, and even has a fast-clicking mechanism avoiding any time loss, allowing you to do other things that were more important, would you be interested in purchasing that unique pen?" (VKK)

Hiring Manager: "Sure, why wouldn't I?"

Candidate: "Great. Well, this pen in my hand is made of a unique fiberglass plastic with a cushioned finger rest, offering a lightweight and soft surface so it doesn't hurt your hand and could even serve as a massage for your finger while the pen gyrates across the page. Additionally, it has a clicking mechanism that's been tested and is proven to even outlive the ink life, so you don't have to worry about the clicker not working, saving you tons of time. And once you try this pen, you'll see that you need it because you're particular about your writing utensils—and this is a very unique pen, given how it's manufactured. Please, take a closer look at it—hold it, write with it—because it's really about how the pen feels to you, and only you can make that determination. Do you see and feel how this pen will meet your needs?" (NAI [Necessity, Away from Pain, Internal Frame of Reference]/VKK)

Hiring Manager: "Actually, yes. I do."

Candidate: "Great. Since you feel that way, the pen you're holding is available for purchase. You mentioned you would pay $15 for an everyday pen that fit your needs—the pen you're holding is $14.99. Would you like to pay with cash or credit card?"

Hopefully you're picking up on the ease of which this skill can be acquired and applied. Let's go again!

CHAPTER 11

Application of the Why Should I...

"Why should we hire you?" is a common interview question. It's not the most dreaded question but it is high on the list of questions those seeking a job abhor answering, and it continues to stay in the rotation.[6] When you apply the techniques of rapport building using the NLP framework, hard questions become easy because you've activated your listening skills and know what questions to ask to help fill in your gaps. When the above question is asked, it usually comes at the end of the interview process. As such, we'll look at a scenario in that vein. Let's take a trip!

Scenario: Recent college graduate interviewing for a junior engineering role.

> **Hiring Manager:** "As you know, we're looking for a junior engineer to fill the role, and that person should ideally have

the skills we previously discussed as well as some real-world experience, maybe a year or two. What questions do you have for me?"

Candidate: "In addition to the skills and years of experience, what type of person are you looking to bring on board?"

Hiring Manager: "We're looking to hire someone who's demonstrated analytical thinking and problem solving while having the emotional intelligence to effectively manage relationships—someone who can focus on the task at hand while being mindful of deadlines, and also someone who works hard and enjoys playing hard."

Candidate: "I'm the person you're looking for. May I ask why the junior engineer role is requesting one to two years of experience? Is that a new requirement?"

Hiring Manager: "We're looking for someone with a little more experience because I've been offered an opportunity for an exciting promotion after finding the right person to fill this role." (Opportunity and Towards Pleasure)

Candidate: "Congratulations! I'm sure you're looking forward to that! How did you settle on the years of experience required?"

Hiring Manager: "Thank you, it's really exciting. Well, my team feels it's optimal that the person we hire not be fresh out of college and have a little real-world experience before stepping into the position, but they'll be comfortable with the person I choose. They trust my judgment." (External)

Candidate: "I see. How much experience did you have when you joined the organization?"

Hiring Manager: "Good question. I came right out of college. Times were different then. The company was just starting and there were many opportunities available. Now, there are fewer opportunities and more available candidates to choose from."

Candidate: "Understandable. At that time, what solidified your decision to join the company?"

Hiring Manager: "Looking back on that, it was the clear picture they gave me about what I would be doing and the future plans of the organization. After considering all of that, it became loud and clear where I should be." (VVA)

Candidate: "Thanks for sharing that."

Hiring Manager: "So please, share with me why we should hire you."

Candidate: "Since you've revealed to me your wonderful opportunity for promotion, it's clear to me why you and your team desire to bring on the right candidate. Success is often determined by vision, focus, determination, and effective communication skills. I have all of those along with the skills to exceed the core function of this role. You want to transition into your new role as quickly as possible knowing you left your colleagues with someone they would've chosen, and like you, I'm before my time. My college professors can attest to my level of wisdom and maturity for my age and when you hire me, I'll show you my focus, dedication, and ability to collaborate with teams effectively. You'll see that even though times have changed, someone with skills and a drive to succeed can make sweet music and put wins on the board for her team. Years of experience are often not a determinant in whether someone succeeds in any organization, as you had no experience and look at you. I represent an opportunity for you to show your colleagues your keen decision-making skills and position yourself to start enjoying your new role sooner rather than later. I can start as early as two weeks from today, unless you and your team would like me to start sooner?" (VVA and OTE)

For your benefit, reassess the examples above, invest the time and dissect them. The "Pen" and "Why Hire" examples, took a sales model from A to Z with some worthwhile stops along the way. The examples built rapport through adequate probing and easily employed the NLP framework to achieve an ideal and effective close.

The more good I put in, the more good I get out.

The above question could easily have been, "Why should I upgrade my software now?" or "Why should I purchase this equipment?" Processes designed for the intended purpose will produce results, but when a framework within a process or a subprocess exists, it's destined and designed to make the outcome more favorable for all parties, irrespective of the subject matter or industry.

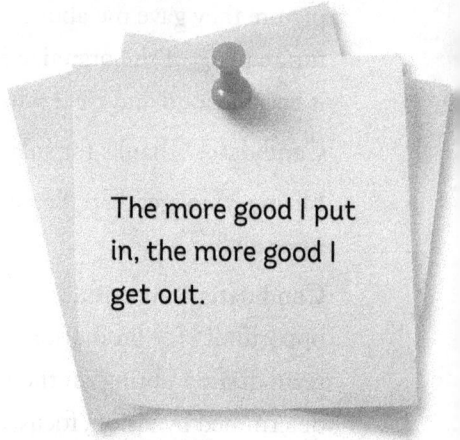

CHAPTER 12

Be the Bridge

Some people view sales in a negative context. These are likely people who've had bad experiences in some aspect of the purchasing cycle. It's unfortunate, but that probably applies to many of us. Sales is a process and requires people in various roles for its existence and sustainability. As with all processes, there's input, work performed, and output. In the sales process, desiring consumers are the input, companies and sales personnel perform some work, and the output is a consumer who has made a purchase.

We're all consumers in one way or another, and where there are consumers, representation of some sort is useful and, oftentimes, imperative. The goal of extraordinary sales professionals should be to leave each prospect or potential prospect with the feeling that they've been usefully served, whether they purchased or not. Exceptional sales professionals should desire to brand themselves in a way that exudes a servant mentality. When you have this mentality, you work to build rapport and meet the product or service gap of your prospect. In accomplishing this goal, there are various tools and models one can consider. However, in my many years of sales and service, I have yet to experience a sales tactic as effective as NLP. It allows the sales professional to dig deep and add tremendous value to the sales cycle.

When NLP is deployed properly, you and/or your team can show a prospect the value of choosing your product or service, allowing him or her to be the decision-maker. NLP allows you to carry the torch 3/4 of the way and let the client finish the sale for you and them.

Most people don't like to be sold to but when you build rapport, understanding how a person best receives information (VAK) and how they're motivated to choose (Meta Program), you're not selling—the prospect is deciding whether to buy. If you did

Am I simply selling or am I serving?

your job effectively, the sale will close with your new customer smiling about the decision **they** made, seeing you as the bridge to something better.

Conclusion

Traditional sales methods can lead to a circuitous process, taking you through highs and lows, peaks and valleys, ups and downs, and roundabouts, as illustrated below. Applying traditional methods could take days, weeks, or even months to turn a lead into a client:

Day—Far Into
The Future

Day 1

When you know how to build rapport more quickly and apply NLP methods as previously mentioned, you'll infuse value into every interaction, convert with ease, and make the distance from prospect to happy client the shortest—a straight (and satisfying) line for you and your client:

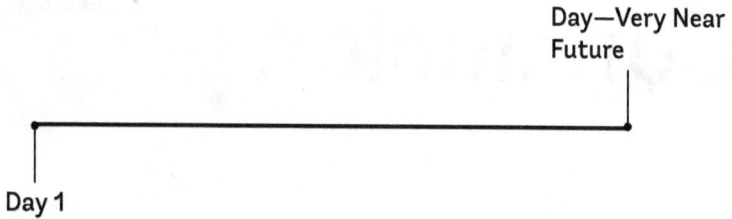

Day—Very Near Future

Day 1

Whether you're selling a car, a multimillion-dollar piece of capital equipment, or a cup of coffee, knowing your audience and showing value is critical to sales success. Value-based selling must start with focusing on what's important to your customer.

Asking the right questions based on NLP and **knowing** how to use the feedback will help tailor the conversation to that unique customer, allowing you to build value that far exceeds the basic features-and-benefits paradigm. Crafting your product offering around how your customer perceives information and makes decisions allows you to build true value and mitigate the path of discounts and rebates.

NLP can be a supplemental tool in your arsenal or your primary tool, as it was ours. Incorporating the abbreviated NLP tactics into our model was priceless. Broad implementation took time, as some employees were stuck in their ways and reluctant to switch over. A transitional phase was anticipated and should also be expected for you and your team.

Success gets attention. The close rate of employees on our team who fully incorporated NLP **was 100 times greater** than those not eager and willing to fully embrace the model. Numbers don't lie, and eventually the entire team adopted NLP fully, resulting in companywide success. If our organization could succeed with the proper and correct adoption of an NLP model that works, so can you and your organization.

You're encouraged to download all the resources at **www.LauriMNelson.com** to aid in your continued skill-building. This book was designed to give you tools that can be employed immediately after reading and offer you quick success with building rapport and closing more sales.

If you or your organization see an opportunity where this training could lift your sales, service, or program development to a new level, please contact us to take advantage of customized Connect & Win Training at **1LauriNelson@gmail.com** and visit **www.LauriMNelson.com** to learn more about what the program will deliver.

If you need to speak with us to discuss your unique situation now, please reach out to us at the email address above with your name and the best phone number to connect with you.

Cheers to your servant and sales success!

ACTION PLAN

_____

_____

_____

_____

_____

_____

_____

_____

_____

_____

_____

_____

_____

_____

_____

_____

_____

_____

KEY CUSTOMER NOTES

REFERENCES

1. *Why Lead-to-Sales Conversion Rates in Life Science Are So Low and What to Do About It.* Marina Hop. Accessed Aug. 4, 2018, http://www.frontlinegenomics.com/opinion/11684/lead-sales-conversion-rates-life-science-low/.

2. *Good Net Promoter Score (NPS): What Is It?* Jamie Yan. Accessed May 22, 2018, https://www.questionpro.com/blog/nps-considered-good-net-promoter-score/.

3. *Neuro-Linguistic Programming (NLP).* Accessed Aug. 4, 2018, https://www.goodtherapy.org/learn-about-therapy/types/neuro-linguistic-programming.

4. Wayne Chung, *Master the NLP Yoga Now* (Kirin International A.G., 2017).

5. *Finding the Right Key.* Tony Robbins. Accessed Feb. 15, 2018, https://www.tonyrobbins.com/leadership-impact/finding-the-right-key/.

6. *Five Interview Questions Job-Seekers Hate to Answer.* Liz Ryan. Accessed Aug. 4, 2018, https://www.forbes.com/sites/lizryan/2016/04/04/five-interview-questions-job-seekers-hate-to-answer/#11fad31d4a28.

ABOUT THE AUTHOR

Lauri Nelson has over 20 years of experience in sales, marketing, program development, and neuro-linguistic language application. She has mastered the art of effective communication, and successfully integrated her program knowledge into several organizations. Lauri has built and helped transform businesses and has trained sales and service professionals to communicate with purpose through deeper insights, goal-focused listening, and active execution based on learned behaviors. Having worked with various organizations, including multiple Fortune 500 companies, Lauri is excited to share her wealth of knowledge and experience with others to help them Connect & Win.